I CHOOSE
Acceptance

I CHOOSE SERIES

ELIZABETH ESTRADA

Copyright 2022 by Elizabeth Estrada - All rights reserved.
Published and printed in the USA.

No part of this publication or the information in it may be quoted or
reproduced in any form by means of printing, scanning, photocopying,
or otherwise without permission of the copyright holder.

I CHOOSE
Acceptance

ELIZABETH ESTRADA

The world is a big, huge place,
With many different kinds of people living in it.
I love meeting all people,
Each one is unique, I'll admit.

Wouldn't it be terrible?
Wouldn't it be bad?
If just one color
Was all that we had?

Differences were made for us to accept,
Not to tolerate.
Our heart was made for love,
Not for hate.

Look inside
And you'll see much more.
Touch someone's heart
And you'll open a door.

Imagine a peaceful world
Where acceptance abounds
A beautiful world
Where laughter's the only sound.

Hope and compassion
Are where it starts
Remember that beyond a face
Is a heart.

To accept is to love
And that is the ultimate test.
When we accept,
It means we are doing our best.

To me, it's so exciting
To be around people of different races.
I love to look around
And see a variety of colored faces.

But I also love to learn of other cultures
Different than mine,
I'm reminded that the world is big
And there's so much to explore when I have the time.

Not everyone is as excited
That people are different than they are,
Some people are mean and hurtful,
They take teasing way too far.

To care for others, no matter their differences,
And embrace variety in the world,
It's called acceptance
And you can choose it whether you are a boy or girl.

Acceptance doesn't only apply
To race or culture of a person,
It's bringing others into your heart
So that the world's conditions do not worsen.

I choose acceptance of other people regardless of
Race, gender or who they choose to love.
Acceptance is the kind of thing
That the world needs much more of.

As you look around a room
And see people unlike you,
Hopefully now that you've learned about acceptance,
You'll know exactly what to do.

Embrace them and their background,
Ask them about their family's history.
Tell them about yours,
Paint a picture with words that they can see.

And know that at our core,
We are really all the same,
Each of us is a human being,
Even if we all go by different names.

www.ingramcontent.com/pod-product-compliance
Lightning Source LLC
Chambersburg PA
CBHW041521070526
44585CB00002B/31